WONDERS!
Our World in Fact and Fiction

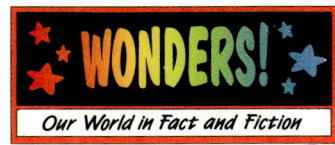

Weather Watch

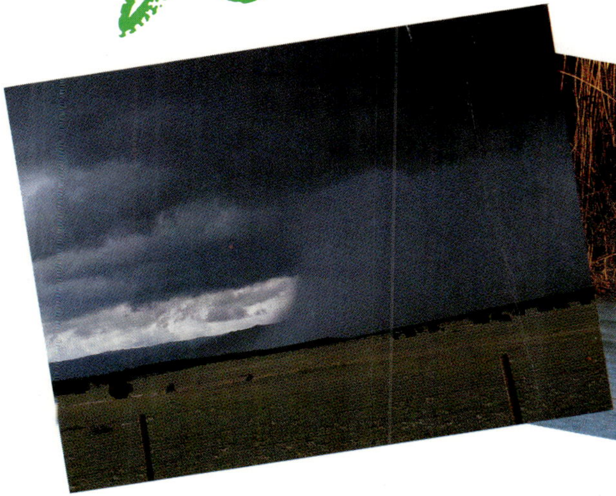

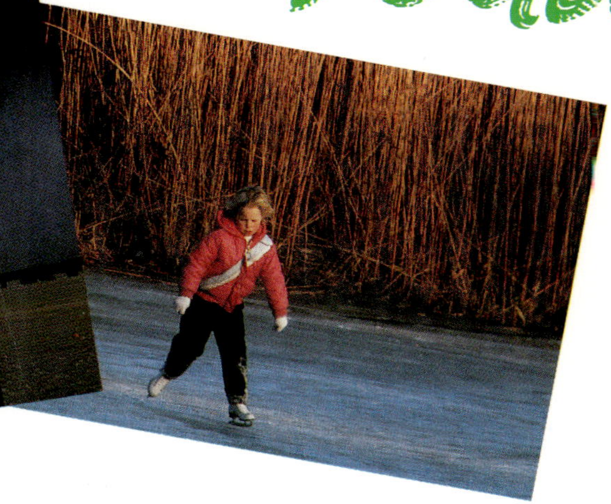

Ina Cumpiano
illustrated with photographs

HAMPTON-BROWN BOOKS
Creative Materials for Active Learning™

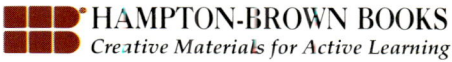

ACKNOWLEDGMENT
We gratefully acknowledge the following:
Wind vane activity on page 15 from 175 SCIENCE EXPERIMENTS TO AMUSE AND AMAZE YOUR FRIENDS by Brenda Walpole. Copyright © 1987 by Grisewood & Dempsey Ltd. Reprinted by permission of Random House, Inc.

Copyright © 1992 Hampton-Brown Books
All rights reserved. No part of this book may be reproduced or transmitted in any form or by any means, electronic or mechanical, including photocopying, recording or by an information storage and retrieval system, without permission in writing from the Publisher.

Hampton-Brown Books
P.O. Box 223220
Carmel, California 93922

Printed in the United States of America
ISBN 1-56334-071-2

92 93 94 95 96 97 98 99 00 01 10 9 8 7 6 5 4 3 2 1

Illustrations: Sharron O'Neil

Photographs: TSW: cover; Frank Cezus/TSW: cover inset 1; Cameron Davidson/TSW: cover inset 2; Superstock/Four-By-Five: 1a, 1b, 8b, 9b, 9c, 16b, 21c; Animals Animals/Earth Scenes: 2a, 2b, 6a, 9a, 12c, 13b, 13c, 14a, 20b, 21a, back cover inset 1; COMSTOCK: 3a, back cover inset 2; Image Bank: 3b, 5a; NASA: 4a; Photo Researchers: 8a, 10a, 12a, 12b, 13a, 14c, 18a, 18b, 19a, 19b, 20c; AllStock: 9d, 20a, 21b; KCBS-TV2: 22b, 23c; Craig Lovell: 24a.

What's everywhere
that it can be—
and yet, it's nothing
you can see?

It's the **air**, of course.

Although air is always around us, you can't see it. But if you were to travel in a space ship, you *would* be able to see the air that surrounds the Earth.

You can't see the air here on Earth, but you can feel it in many ways.

When you feel the wind blowing on your face, what you are feeling is moving air.

When the rain gets you wet, what you are feeling is the moisture of the air.

Hands On

If you want to "see" the air, you can do the following experiment. Put some water in a glass bowl. Add some tempera paint. Then put a drinking glass upside down in the water. What happens?

When you are hot in the summer or cold in the winter, what you are feeling is the temperature of the air.

The temperature, movement, and moisture of the air change constantly, and this is what causes the weather.

Hot Days, Cold Days

Sun and Earth

Near the equator, where sunlight strikes directly, it is hot.

It is colder near the poles. Because the surface of the earth is curved, sunlight does not strike directly, and the rays spread out over a larger area.

All Around the World

Some places are almost always hot. Others are almost always cold. In most places it is cold some of the time and hot some of the time.

In Lappland, in the north of Finland, winters are harsh and last a full nine months. Reindeer provide food, and their hides are used to make clothing, tents, and blankets.

Tahiti is an island on the Pacific Ocean. Its very warm climate allows people to wear very light clothing almost all the time.

In Greenland, near the North Pole, the Eskimo, or Inuit, people wear clothes made of animal skins to protect them from the extreme cold.

Summer heat in the Moroccan desert is very intense. People must wear clothing that protects them from the burning sun.

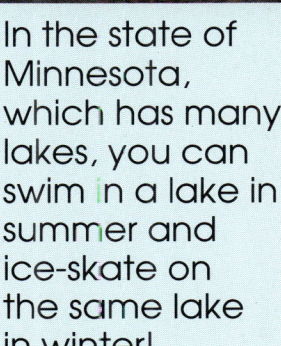

In the state of Minnesota, which has many lakes, you can swim in a lake in summer and ice-skate on the same lake in winter!

Thermometers measure the temperature of the air.

Inside a thermometer there is a liquid—mercury or alcohol—which rises when it's hot and falls when it's cold. It may rise and fall several times during a day. The weather is always changing!

mercury or alcohol

Windy Days

cooler air hot air

As you know, air temperature changes. When air heats up, it rises. Cooler air then comes and fills the place that the rising hot air left empty. This movement is what produces the wind.

The wind can be our friend, . . .

You can have fun with the help of the wind.

The wind can help you go from one place to another.

The wind helps produce electrical energy.

... but sometimes it is destructive.

A tornado, which is like a funnel of strong wind, can cause a lot of damage in a short time.

The winds of a hurricane can destroy buildings and injure people.

The wind can spread the flames of a fire.

The wind can blow from any direction. A wind is named according to the direction it **comes from**. For example, the north wind comes from the north.

In our part of the earth, north winds are colder and south winds are warmer. Winds that come from the sea or pass over lakes and rivers carry moisture and rain.

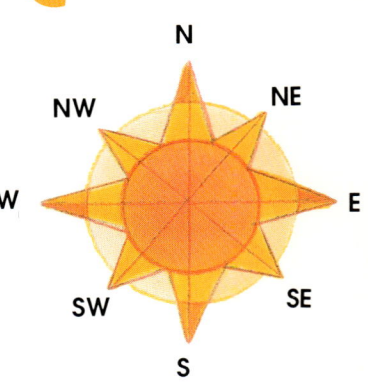

Compass rose

A compass rose shows the directions the wind can come from.

Hands On

Get together with three classmates and make a weather vane to see which direction the wind is coming from.

- Make the arrow from a straw and two triangles of cardboard. Make the rear triangle a little larger. Push a pin through the middle of the straw and then into the eraser of a pencil.

- Put a lump of modeling clay on a cardboard square. Stick a paper cup upside-down on it. Then, punch the pencil with the straw through the bottom of the cup and into the clay.

- Write the letters $N, S, E,$ and W on the cardboard and take the weather vane outdoors, orienting it so that the N is toward the north.

Watch the weather vane move. The wind is coming from the direction that the arrow is pointing.

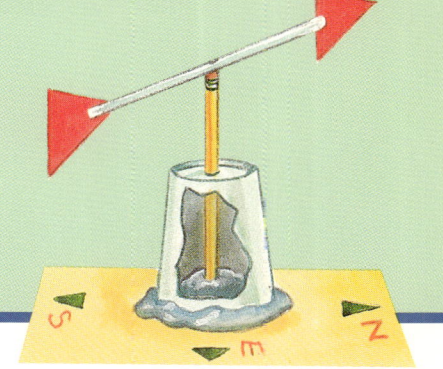

Hands On

The next time it rains, you can "trap" a few raindrops.

- Let a few drops of rain fall on a plate of flour.
- Let the flour dry completely.
- Put it in a strainer and sift it. The little balls of flour that remain are the size of rain drops.

Rain! Rain!

Whether it's drizzle, downpour, or a cloud in the sky, all the moisture in the air is part of a **cycle**, or circle. In the water cycle, the earth's water is used again and again.

The Water Cycle

The sun heats the oceans, the lakes, and the land, and a large amount of water rises into the air in the form of invisible **water vapor**.

As it rises, this vapor cools and turns into clouds, which are made up of tiny droplets of water.

This liquid falls from the clouds in the form of rain or snow and returns once more to the oceans, the lakes, and the land. Then the cycle repeats.

Not all moisture in the air falls in the form of rain.

Fog is a cloud so low that it touches the ground. It is very hard to see when there is heavy fog.

The balls of ice that make up hail vary in size. This photo shows some that are almost as big as a baseball. They can cause a lot of damage.

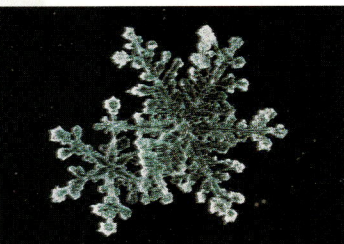

Snow is made up of tiny ice crystals. As they fall through the air, they stick together to form snowflakes.

THAT'S A FACT!

The Kobuk Eskimos of Alaska live where it is cold almost all year round. Since a great amount of snow falls where they live, they have many words to describe snow.

annui: falling snow
api: snow that is on the ground
pukak: a light, loose layer of snow
qali: snow piled up on tree branches
siqoq: snow whirling in the wind
upsik: snow that the wind has compacted and made hard

We need the moisture in the air, . . .

Rain waters the crops . . .

. . . and gives us the fresh water we use every day.

Snow can be fun.

. . . but too much moisture can be harmful.

If too much rain falls, rivers overflow and cause flooding.

When ice forms on airplanes, they cannot fly.

Ships cannot navigate well when there is fog, because it is hard to see.

21

It's important to know what the weather's going to be, so you know what to wear or whether to take an umbrella. People who study the weather and try to predict what the weather will be are called **meteorologists.**

They give weather reports on television using maps and symbols like these.

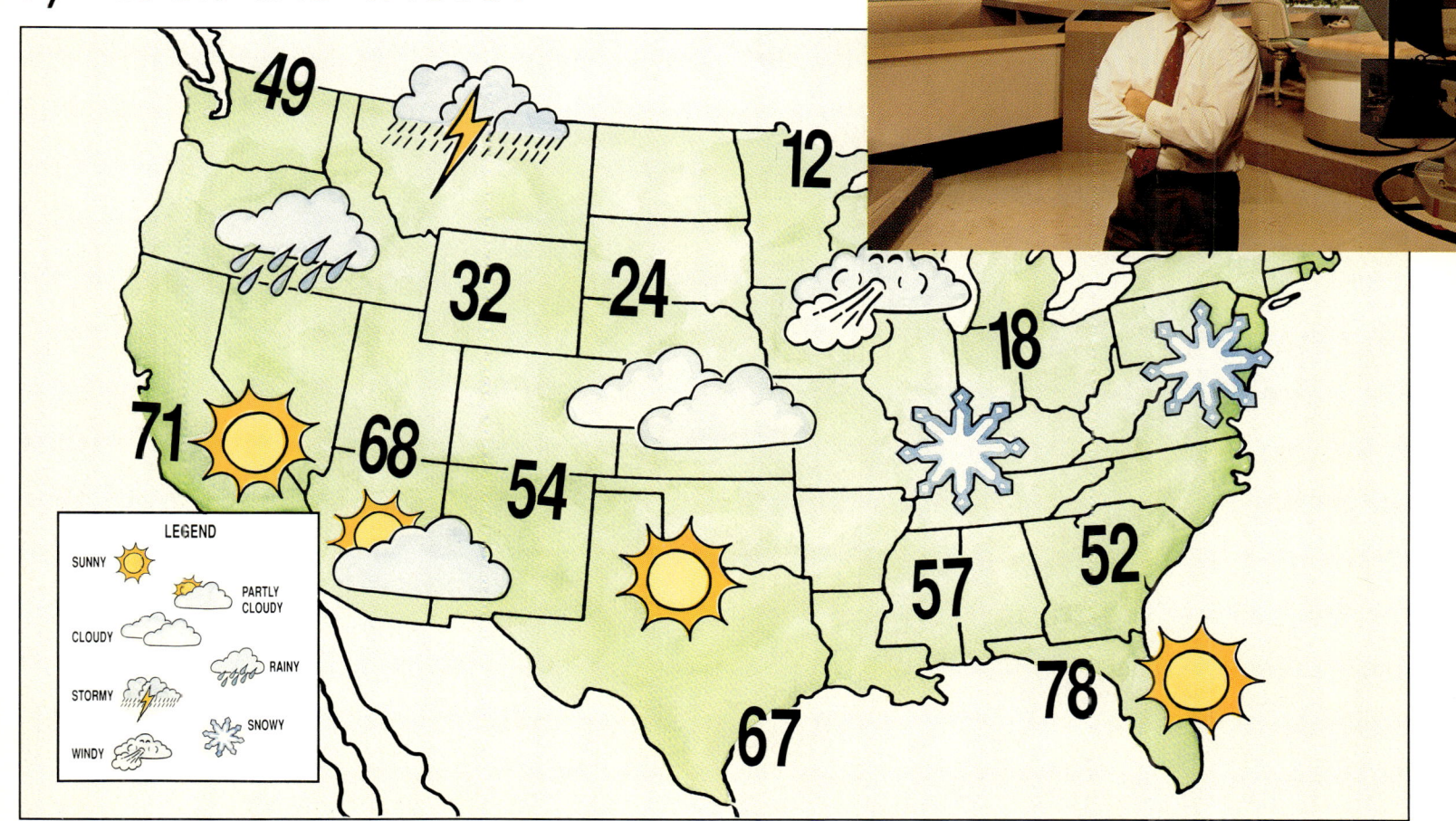

Maybe you can't predict tomorrow's weather. But you can keep an eye on the weather by observing the temperature, wind, and moisture in the air.

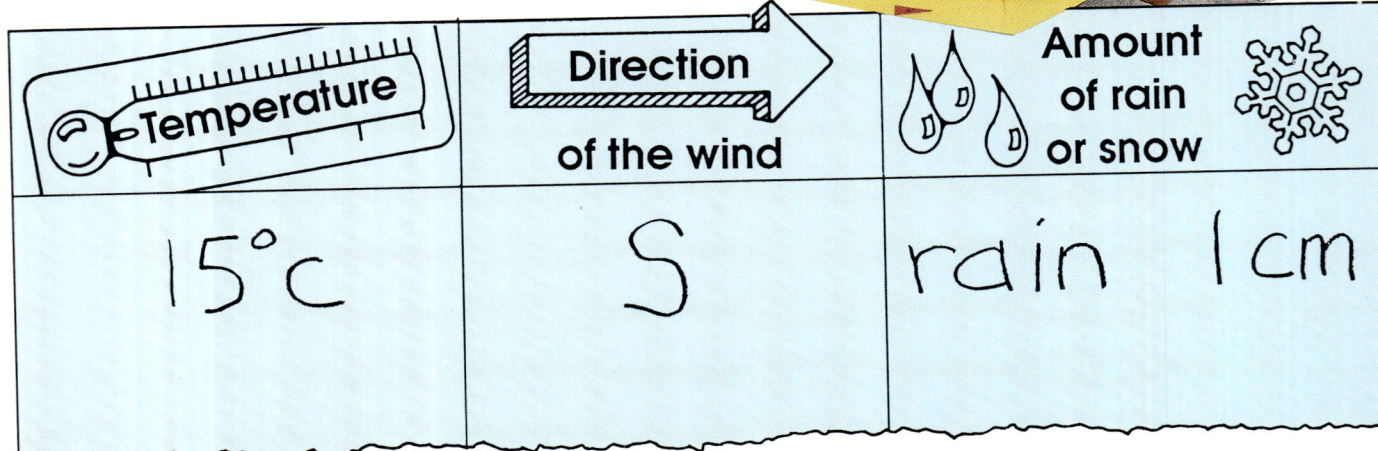

Temperature	Direction of the wind	Amount of rain or snow
15°c	S	rain 1 cm

Rain, or shine? How's the weather today where you live?